CONTENTS

Introduction

What is it that makes humans different from the other animals? There are many different answers to this question, but one is that we have formed special ways of living together in societies, which are quite different from those of even our closest animal relatives such as gorillas and chimpanzees. Human societies involve sharing resources such as food, caring for others, producing imaginative works like paintings and sculptures and being able to ask questions about the unknown, such as what happens after we die.

One of the first examples of this was a very early discovery – the use and control of fire. When our early ancestors learned about fire, hundreds of thousands of years ago, they discovered how to make food taste better by cooking, how to keep themselves warm and even how to scare away dangerous creatures that were afraid of the flames. It was one of the most important discoveries in human history. It also brought people together – when they gathered together around a fire, sharing their food and warmth, our ancestors took the first step on the road to civilization.

Early people soon became aware of illness and death. They disposed of their dead carefully, arranging their bodies in graves and often burying items, called grave goods, with them, so that they

IDEAS AND INVENTIONS

LIFE AND DEATH

Pushing the Boundaries of Knowledge

Philip Wilkinson

Illustrated by Robert Ingpen

Chrysalis Children's Books

First published in the UK in 2005 by
Chrysalis Children's Books
An imprint of Chrysalis Books Group Plc,
The Chrysalis Building, Bramley Road, London W10 6SP

ISBN 1 84458 213 2

British Library Cataloguing in Publication Data
for this book is available from the British Library.

Editorial Manager: Joyce Bentley
Senior Editor: Rasha Elsaeed
Series Editor: Jon Richards
Editorial Assistant: Camilla Lloyd
Designed by: Tall Tree Ltd
Cover Make-up: Wladek Szechter

Previously published in four volumes for Dragon's World *Caves to Cathedrals, Science & Power, Scrolls to Computers* and *Wheels to Rockets*.

Printed in China

10 9 8 7 6 5 4 3 2 1

would have things to use in the afterlife. So ideas about religion and life after death began very early. The first cave paintings were probably made during religious ceremonies, perhaps as rituals performed before people went out hunting, in the hope that they would bring back plenty of food.

Religion also played a large part in early medicine. People hoped to be cured of their illnesses by making offerings to the gods. At the same time, they also made vital discoveries about plants and other substances that could help cure their illnesses. All sorts of traditional plant-based medicines have since been discovered to contain chemicals that really do help us get better.

Modern researchers have added to this traditional knowledge. Their discoveries began with more scientific ways of studying the human body and how it works. They have also brought safer methods of carrying out operations, anaesthetics to make these procedures painless and vaccinations that have virtually eliminated many diseases that once killed millions of people – a triumphant end to the story of sharing and caring that began thousands of years ago around a glowing hearth.

PHILIP WILKINSON

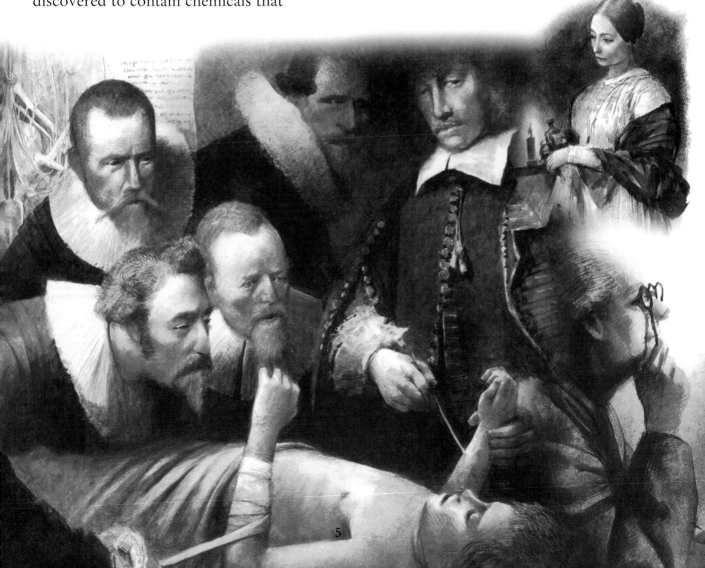

MAKING FIRE

By harnessing fire, people began to control one of the forces of nature. Now, they could make night into day, and keep warm even in the coldest temperatures.

As early hominids began to move out of Africa and spread around the world, they found that some climates were too cold for them to live in. To survive there, they needed to make another important discovery: the use of fire. The first hominid to use fire was probably *Homo erectus* who was more intelligent than earlier species. Archaeologists have discovered evidence of fire at the *Homo erectus* site at Choukoutien in China. Ashes, charred bones and charcoal have been found in a large cave where people lived 300,000 to

400,000 years ago. The bones, mainly of deer, were probably the remains of meals that had been cooked over the fire.

People had watched fires started by natural causes such as lightning for many thousands of years before they first thought of making fire for themselves.

△ *Lightning was a natural cause of fire.*

▷ *Turning a stick between the hands was one method of making fire, but the stick had to be pressed hard against a piece of wood at the same time. The bow drill was a more efficient method because it made the stick spin faster and caused more friction between the stick and the hearth.*

People were probably terrified of fire at first, just as other animals were. As they got used to seeing fires, they realized that they would come to no harm if they took care. Fires gave off tremendous heat as they raged across the countryside, and they lit up the night sky. People began to see that fire's light and heat could be useful. They discovered that they could light a bundle of twigs in a forest fire and carry the flaming twigs back to the cave or camp where more wood could be set alight to provide warmth and light. If the fire was kept stoked up with fuel, it would burn for as long as they wanted it.

COOKING FOOD

Fire made a great difference to people's lives. For the first time, they could venture into places that were too cold to live in without it. They could also make their food tastier by cooking. Early hominids ate meat before they discovered fire, so they must have eaten it raw. Raw meat is tough and difficult to chew, but cooking makes it tender. This fact was probably discovered by accident. Someone may have dropped some food into the fire and found to their surprise that it tasted far better afterwards, or perhaps they ate meat from an animal killed in a forest fire.

Early people often ate meat that had been roasted on a stick over the flames. Sometimes, food was cooked more slowly in the embers of the fire. They may also have wrapped meat in a thick layer of clay and leaves to make a sort of oven which could be put in the fire.

Finding food was a hazardous task. On some days, the hunters would catch nothing. On other days, they might kill an animal that provided far too much meat for one meal. Before the discovery of fire, they had to throw away what they could not eat, or leave it lying where they

▽ *The camp fire not only provided warmth and light, but also kept wild animals at bay.*

8

▽ *A curved lens can concentrate the sun's rays on to a small area. The temperature becomes so high that it sets the dry grass alight.*

In California, large 'fire lenses' have been found which date from between 1.8 million and 10,000 years ago.

had found it. Fire allowed people to smoke meat and fish to store it for times when supplies were scarce.

NIGHT LIGHT

Fire lit up caves and underground passages where daylight never penetrated, so people could begin to live in these dark places. Before the discovery of fire, people could not do anything after darkness had fallen. Now, when the day's hunting was over, they could sit and make tools by firelight. The points of spears and arrows could be charred in the fire to make them stronger.

Homo erectus was capable of a primitive form of speech by this time, so perhaps people sat around the fire and discussed the day's hunting or where they would go to hunt the next day. Gathering around the fire at the end of the day may have been the start of communal living.

A camp or cave fire also gave the people protection. Early people were under constant threat of attack from wild animals. A fire burning through the night kept animals away. They might skulk in the shadows, but they would not come into its light. Fire in a cave drove out wild animals that lived there. Forest fires could also be useful in the search for food. Terrified animals rushed out of the flames towards the hunters who were waiting for them. The fresh undergrowth that grew back after a fire provided more plant food for animals and people.

MAKING FIRE

People had now learned to make use of natural fires, but it was not very convenient to wait for a forest fire every time heat or light were needed. Perhaps people noticed sparks flying when they were chipping flint tools. If a glowing

spark fell on to dry grass, it could set it alight. Once people realized that they could start a fire by producing a spark in this way, they could light a fire whenever they wanted to. Archaeologists have found stones which they think were used to start fires. Lumps of flint which would not have been suitable for making tools had obviously been banged with other stones to start a fire. Striking flints together was fairly efficient, but using a flint to strike a rock containing a yellow vein of iron pyrites was eventually found to produce better sparks.

People may also have noticed that two dry branches brushing together in the wind sometimes caused sparks. Perhaps they decided to imitate this by rubbing sticks together. Then, they began to devise more efficient ways of creating fire. One of these was to press a round stick hard against a flat piece of wood and rotate it quickly between the palms of the hands. The bow drill was later used to turn the stick very fast and produce a flame more quickly.

FIREPLACES AND HEARTHS

Early people moved around, hunting and gathering plant food. They followed the same route each year, stopping at places where they knew the hunting was good. At night, they found a cave or made a shelter where they could sleep. Sometimes they stayed in one camp for a few days before moving on. The earliest fires would simply have been a pile of sticks in the cave or outside the shelter.

When people began to build huts, they made permanent fireplaces. The earliest

◁ *The hunters brought back the animals they had killed that day. The meat was cut up and roasted on the fire. Smaller pieces could be pierced with sticks and held in the flames.*

FIRE AND FOOD

Fire made a difference to the way in which people developed. Early hominids had large, flat molars set in heavy jaws, so that they could chew tough raw meat. Once people began to cook their meat, their teeth and jaws became smaller. Early hominids also had large canine teeth which they used for tearing food, as apes and monkeys do. The canine teeth of *Homo erectus* were smaller.

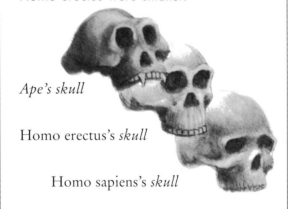

Ape's skull

Homo erectus's *skull*

Homo sapiens's *skull*

were shallow pits, sometimes surrounded by stones. Later, people built hearths with a large flat stone as the base and raised sides to hold the fire and ashes.

Wood was the main fuel for these fires and at first people used it for both heating and light. Gradually though, they began to make special lamps which burned oil made from animal fat. Some lamps were made from a large bone with a hollow in it. Others were cut from soft rock such as sandstone. The dish of the lamp was filled with the fat, and a wick made of moss was added. The wick burned until all the fat had been used up.

The discovery of fire made a huge difference to the lives of early people. Not only did they now have warmth and light, but their way of life began to change too, from their diet to the hours they slept and woke.

LIFE & DEATH

*As survival became easier for people,
they began to consider the world around them.
They searched for causes and meanings to
problems or events in their lives, such as birth,
death, disease and bad harvests.*

L ife was hard for the early
hominids. The search for food
and shelter was so demanding that
it left little time for anything else.
At some point, about 80,000 years
ago, some of these early people found
time to establish rituals and ceremonies.
The earliest of these were concerned with
burying the dead. Animals do not bury
their dead and the earliest people did not
either. The first burials must have
occurred after people had begun to think
about things other than hunting and
keeping warm.

THE FIRST GRAVES

We do not know exactly when the first
burials happened. Many ancient graves
have been discovered but there may be
older ones which have yet to be found.

△ *Birth and death were two of the puzzles
which led people to develop religious beliefs.*

▷ *People probably decorated their bodies with
paint and wore special costumes for early rituals.
Music and dancing would have been included.
Some early ceremonial sites, such as the huge
standing stones of Stonehenge in England, show
that people attached great importance to
religion, but we can only guess at the exact
content of these ceremonies.*

ANIMAL MAGIC

Animals were part of Neanderthal people's beliefs and rituals, probably because they were such an important part of life. A stone box found in a cave in Switzerland was filled with the skulls of cave bears. Bear's limb bones were placed around the walls. Other examples of rituals featuring cave bears have been found in France, Germany and the former Yugoslavia.

One of the earliest settlements in Europe was at Lepenski Vir on the banks of the River Danube. The community dated from about 5000 BC. Strange heads carved in stone have been found near the centre of each house. The faces have staring eyes and thick, down-turned lips and seem to represent fish gods. The people may have worshipped fish gods because the river provided much of their food.

Goats were important sources of meat, milk and skins to early people, and often became important symbols in the first religions. Goats were represented in the early religious festivals of Greece. These ceremonies gradually evolved into theatre as we know it. The word 'tragedy', which is used to describe some plays, comes from the Greek word 'tragoidia' which means 'goat-song'.

As far as we know, Neanderthal people were the first to bury their dead. They seem to have performed ritual ceremonies which suggest that they had some religious beliefs by this time.

Graves have been found in the earth floors of caves where Neanderthal people lived. The graves are shallow, but even a shallow grave must have taken a long time and a lot of effort to dig with simple stone tools and digging sticks. The body was often placed on its side, with the knees drawn up to the chin, as though the person were asleep. Some bodies were buried with tools, so the Neanderthals may have believed in an after-life in which people needed their earthly possessions with them.

A grave found at Teshik-Tash in Uzbekistan contained the skeleton of a small boy. The boy, who had died when he was eight or nine years old, was buried in a shallow grave in a cave high in the mountains. His head was surrounded by pairs of horns from the Siberian ibex, a goat which still lives in this region. Perhaps these animals were an important source of food and skins for the people who lived there. The bones were arranged like a crown around the boy's head, suggesting that his burial involved some sort of ceremony.

GIFTS FOR THE AFTER-LIFE

It is difficult for us to piece together information about early burials. The graves that have been discovered show that different groups of people had different ideas and customs. Bodies have been positioned in various ways in the graves. Some people were buried with nothing, others had tools with them. Some bodies were buried with food and cooking vessels, perhaps for their journey to the after-life.

▽ *It is likely that music, dance and theatre all developed from ancient religious ceremonies. Performances were probably intended to honour or thank the gods, or to keep away evil spirits. Here, Native American shamans perform a ritual with poisonous snakes.*

These graves do give us some clues about people's lives, however. A mountain cave at Shanidar in Iraq contains the grave of a man who died about 60,000 years ago. The man was about 40 when he died, which was a long life in those days. He lived at a time when all men were expected to hunt, however his arm and shoulder were badly deformed.

He could not have hunted with a useless arm, so his companions must have looked after him and found extra food to feed him. These people seem to have learned to care about others. When this man died, his body was laid on branches and scattered with flowers from the hillsides. Some of these flowers have been known for their healing properties since ancient times. Perhaps the Neanderthals believed the flowers would heal the man in his after-life.

Archaeologists have found some evidence of ancient musical instruments, so religious ceremonies may have involved music and dancing. People played bone flutes and pipes, rattled bracelets made from small pieces of bone or tusk and beat drums.

The earliest drums were large, flat animal bones which were banged with a bone or antler. Drums were also made from wood or bone with skin stretched across them.

EARLY GODS

When early people began to think about the world around them, they found it puzzling and frightening. They knew nothing about science and could not explain why the weather changed, why food was sometimes plentiful and sometimes scarce, and why strange and disastrous things sometimes happened. The only explanation they could find was that everything was controlled by invisible gods. Early gods were often represented by animals or other symbols. The earliest gods worshipped in Egypt date from before the first nomads settled on the banks of the Nile. They often took the form of animals or birds such as lions, monkeys or crocodiles.

The gods and their mysterious ways became even more crucial when farming developed. Farmers depended on the weather and the environment for their survival, as they do today. If the crops failed, there would be no food. The crops could fail because the rains did not come, or because there was too much rain. Many things could happen between

▽ *In many cultures throughout the world, food was offered to the gods to thank them for providing a good harvest.*

sowing the seeds and reaping the harvest. Early farmers believed that everything depended on pleasing the gods. Their own actions could please the gods or make them angry. If the gods were angry, the crops would not grow. Many early gods represented the weather, the soil and even the crops themselves.

PLEASING THE GODS

The Sumerians farmed the fertile valley between the Tigris and Euphrates rivers, in what is now Iraq, between about 4000 and 3000 BC. By about 3500 BC, they had built up a sophisticated civilization with large cities. The early Sumerians believed that their only reason for being on the Earth was to please the gods. When they were not praying in the temples, they left statues of themselves to pray for them in their absence.

Most of the prayers of these early peoples were concerned with the weather. They prayed to rain gods for rain, and to earth gods for rich soil and successful crops. Many religions had a sun god who was the most important because all life depended on the sun rising each day. After a successful harvest, people gave thanks by making offerings to the gods. Harvest festivals are still held today.

In ancient Greece, festivals of song and dance were performed in honour of the gods. Speaking parts were gradually introduced and then whole plays were written about the gods. People wore costumes and masks to show the characters they were playing. These religious festivals were the earliest form of theatre. All modern theatre has its roots in these ancient rituals.

△ *Many early religions made statues or 'totems' of their gods.*

17

THE FIRST ART

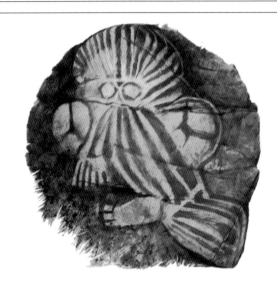

*Once early people had learned
the skills they needed for survival, they
began to look around them and record the
things they saw as pictures and models.*

Human beings have evolved over four million years, but our own direct ancestors, *Homo sapiens sapiens*, appeared only 35,000 years ago. The period from the emergence of *Homo sapiens sapiens* to the time when people began to settle in groups and farm the land is known as the Old Stone Age. The people of the Old Stone Age were hunter-gatherers who had spread from Africa, which is thought to be the birthplace of the first humans.

They had moved all over the world, to Europe, Asia, Australia and the Americas.

These people could make a variety of tools and had learned to light a fire and to build simple shelters. Once they had learned how to keep themselves alive, they began to express themselves by drawing the things they saw around them. This was the first art.

Some of the earliest art appears on the walls of caves where people sheltered at night. Paintings, engravings and carvings show the animals that people hunted. The most common are bison, deer, oxen and horses, but there are also paintings of

△ *Owl wall-painting from northern Australia.*

lions, bears, mammoths, birds and fish in some of the caves.

Why did people start to paint the walls of caves in this way? Was it simply decoration, meant to represent the world around them in pictures, or was it part of some ceremony or ritual? And how did these early artists realize that they could draw, when no one had done so before?

△ *Some pictures were engraved on top of each other in a confusing criss-cross of lines. Sometimes it is still possible to see the outline of an animal.*

SEEING SHAPES

Creating art is part of the human instinct. Small children start to draw simple images from an early age and these become more realistic as they gain greater understanding of the world around them. The ability to draw seems to have evolved as people became more advanced.

▽ *A cave painting of an animal hunt.*

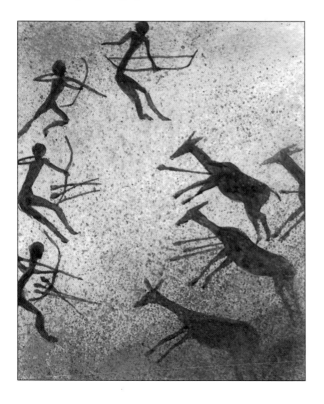

Perhaps it began as they looked around the caves they sheltered in. The insides of the caves were dark and mysterious. People only had the light of primitive lamps to brighten the gloom.

At first, they may have simply begun to see shapes suggested by bumps and patterns in the rock, in the same way that we can sometimes see shapes in clouds when we look up at the sky. Maybe an outline in the rock suggested a mammoth or a deer, and someone decided to improve on nature by scratching in more detail. From there, they could move on to drawing the complete animal and to shaping it in other ways, such as modelling with clay, or carving bone or antler.

Examples of early art have been found in Africa, Asia, the Americas and Australia, but the finest evidence comes from Europe, particularly from caves in France and Spain. There are examples of 'portable' art in the caves, such as carvings in stone, bone and wood, engravings on pieces of stone and bone, and models moulded in clay. One of the most famous clay models is the pair of bison in a cave at Le Tuc d'Audoubert in France. Each animal is almost a metre long, about one-sixth of its real size.

DRAWING ON THE WALLS

On the walls themselves, paintings or engravings are carved into the rock wall. The engravings are sometimes difficult to make out because they have not been carved very deeply. The artists would have needed a range of tools to carry out

△ The artists of the Ice Age used sticks to mix their paints and often put it on the walls with their bare hands. They produced some of the finest cave paintings. Often a whole range of different subjects was represented in a cave.

the carving. To carve fine lines, they used a tool with a sharp point and edge, called a 'burin', and a sharp pointed tool called an 'awl', usually used for piercing hides. Larger, stronger tools such as flint blades and hammers could be used for chipping away bigger pieces of rock.

Some of the most beautiful work is the painting. These early artists used natural materials to make their paints. Ochre is a kind of earth made up of clay and other minerals. It provided red, yellow and brown pigments, and charcoal provided black. No evidence of blue or green paint has been found. The pigments were mixed with water to make paint which

was put on the wall with the artist's hands or with a twig or stick or a brush made from animal hair. Some pictures were a mixture of carving and painting, making use of natural cracks and bumps in the wall. Artists also used a simple stencilling technique. Someone placed his hand against the wall and the artist sprayed paint on to it. When the hand was taken away, its shape was left on the wall. The paint was probably sprayed on with a simple blowpipe made of bone.

MAGIC RITUALS

But what were these pictures all about? People are hardly ever shown in them. When pictures do include people, they are often wearing masks, animal skins and antlers on their heads. These could have been disguises for hunting, but there is nothing to show that the cave paintings were about hunting itself, so it is more

THE FIRST ART

▽ *In ancient times, sometimes giant figures of animals or men were carved into the ground, so that they could be seen from a long way off.*

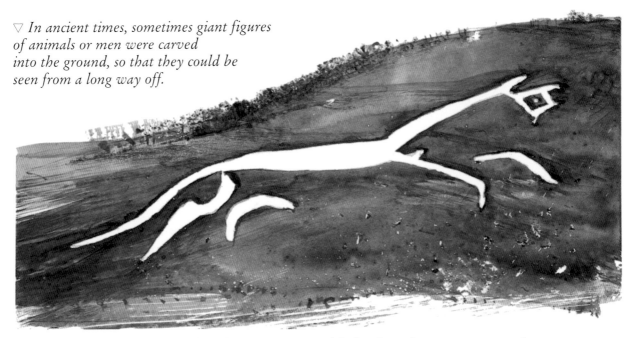

▽ *Some of the best examples of prehistoric art come from Europe. From left to right:*
1 *Charging bison, wall painting, Altamira, Spain, c. 20,000 BC*
2 *Venus of Willendorf, limestone carving, Germany, c. 30,000 BC*
3 *Female figure, ivory carving, central Europe, c. 20,000 BC*
4 *Head of girl, ivory carving, Brassempouy, France, c. 20,000 BC*
5 *Female figure, carving, Germany, c. 20,000 BC*
6 *Staff or spear thrower, antler carving, southern France, c. 20,000 BC*
7 *Statue, stone carving, St Sernin, France, c. 3000 BC*

likely that they were part of some religious ritual. The paintings are often in parts of caves that are very hard to reach, hidden away and dark. The artists would have needed ladders to get to them. Simple ladders were probably made from a small tree trunk with the branches trimmed down. The artists would also have needed lights to work by, but they chose to paint here rather than on walls nearer the mouth of the cave.

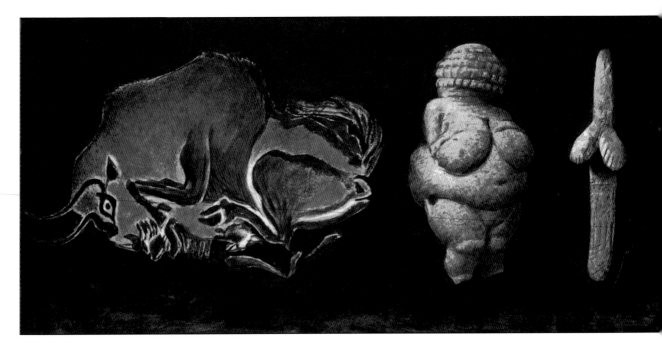

SUCCESSFUL HUNTING

The fact that the paintings were hidden away like this suggests that the caves may have been used for secret rituals. Perhaps the artists simply felt that drawing pictures of animals would make the hunt more successful, or perhaps they were drawn as part of a ceremony that took place before the hunt.

Some of the animals have been painted with arrows stuck in them, others look as though they have been attacked with stones. Perhaps the people believed that this would help them to kill real animals. Or perhaps the artists drew animals to make sure that their numbers increased so that there would always be plenty to hunt.

We cannot really know the reasons behind the paintings. Maybe, like art today, they were carried out for different reasons. Some may have been the work of artists trying to paint what they saw around them. Others may have had religious significance. Whatever their reasons for their paintings and carvings, artists went on adding to the cave art for about 15,000 years.

HUMAN FIGURES

Most early art portrays animals but some statues of women have been found as well. The most famous of these are the 'Venus' figures. They all have large breasts, a rounded stomach and massive thighs. Perhaps prehistoric man's idea of female beauty was a large, curvaceous figure, or maybe these figures are meant to represent goddesses of the day.

One of the best-known is the plump, well-rounded figure of the Venus of Willendorf which was carved in Germany about 32,000 years ago. The Venus of Laussel was carved in the Dordogne area of France at about the same time.

Other female statues are slim or seem to be of older women. Archaeologists are not sure what these figures represent. Some female figures have been found in special pits in what were once the floors of huts. They may have been models of the inhabitants' ancestors, as some early people worshipped their ancestors.

CURES & REMEDIES

*Most of the medical practices of long ago
seem barbarous or ridiculous today,
but some have proved valuable to
modern medicine.*

Early people knew nothing about the bacteria and viruses that cause disease. A wound caused by a cut or a fall was easy enough to understand, and people could see what had happened if they were ill after eating food that was bad or poisonous. However, the sudden onset of a mystery illness was not so easily explained. The only answer early people could find to this problem was that disease must be caused by evil spirits, perhaps because the gods were angry with the people.

MEDICINE MEN

Early cures took the form of rituals to appease the gods or drive out evil spirits. A medicine man or witch doctor would put on an elaborate ceremonial costume and dance to cast out spirits or ask forgiveness of the gods. These methods have nothing to do with medicine as we know it today, but they often seemed to work. If the illness was not too serious,

△ *Witch doctors performed rituals intended to drive evil spirits out of the bodies of the sick.*

▷ *Simple medicines were made from plants from the earliest times.*

the person may have recovered naturally and believed their recovery was due to the medicine man. Also, when people had faith in these forms of medicine, they believed they were going to get better, and their positive thinking helped to give them the strength to recover.

Early medicine was not all ritual and magic. Medicine men gradually learned about plants which could be helpful in curing disease. There were also early attempts at surgery. Prehistoric skulls with holes bored in them have been discovered in various parts of the world. This operation, which is called 'trepanning', was probably carried out with a pointed flint tool and was intended to allow evil spirits to escape from the brain. The treatment must have been agony, but we know that people survived it because many of the skulls show that the holes in the bone had healed.

SYMPTOMS AND DIAGNOSES

As early civilizations developed, people became more organized in their approach to medicine. They still believed that everything was controlled by the gods, but there was some training in the administration of plant remedies. Remedies were written down and a record kept of patients' case histories. Doctors also began to diagnose illnesses by examination and asking the patients questions about their symptoms. In ancient Egypt, doctors were priests who had had medical training. Being a doctor was often a family profession, with fathers passing their medical knowledge to their sons. There were different doctors for different parts of the body. The pharaoh even had a different doctor for each of his eyes!

Egyptian doctors followed many practices carried out by doctors today. They took the patient's pulse and felt their body temperature, though this was simply a matter of feeling whether the person was too hot. They did not know precisely what the pulse or the body temperature should be, but they learned to recognise what was normal. The Egyptians also used splints to mend broken bones and gave patients a wide range of herbal medicines. In Egypt, doctors were paid by the government and

▷ *Many herbs have medicinal properties, and herbal remedies have been used for centuries. Today, scientists can extract the useful chemicals in these plants and make them into drugs. For example, the foxglove (centre left) contains substances which can be used to treat heart disease. The plant ephedra (centre) can be used to make ephedrine to treat low blood pressure and asthma.*

▷ *The four humours were supposed to affect the character as well as health. People governed by air (top left) were supposed to be cheerful; fire (top right) made people hot-tempered; water (bottom left) made them sluggish; and earth (bottom right) made them melancholy.*

HERBAL REMEDIES

Today, many people have begun to use the herbal cures that were used in the past. Some of the most common herbs have useful properties.

Garlic crushed in oil and rubbed on the chest is good for congestion.

Peppermint tea is good for hiccups.

Sage leaves rubbed on an insect bite will relieve the itching.

Rosemary soaked in oil will help to heal bruises.

△ *Hippocrates, father of modern medicine.*

Galen, the great Roman physician.

patients were treated free if they were travelling or fighting in a war. Although the Egyptians' methods were quite modern in some ways, they still relied on the gods to help out, and their knowledge of the human body was not very great. Cures involved praying to the gods, particularly those with healing properties. People thought that if they made offerings to the priests at the temples of these gods, it would help them to stay in good health.

THE HUMOURS

The ancient Greeks were the first people to practise a form of medicine which had nothing to do with religious beliefs. Greek physicians realized that some common symptoms always appear together and that certain medicines brought relief for these symptoms.

The first man to put forward this new theory was Hippocrates (fifth century BC), who lived on the Greek island of Kos. Hippocrates is still said to be the father of medicine. He did not know much about the human body and how it is made up, but he believed that four elements, fire, air, water and earth, made up the universe and that they had their equivalents in the human body. These were the four 'humours', blood, phlegm, yellow bile and black bile. These substances had to be kept balanced in the body. If the balance was disrupted and one of the humours began to dominate the others, a person became ill.

The humours theory was incorrect but Hippocrates' methods of diagnosis by careful observation was the basis of medicine for centuries. He was also right about imbalances in the body causing illness and some of his treatments made good sense. For example, if a patient had a raging fever, fire was said to be the element in control of his body, and the balance had to be restored by lowering his temperature.

ROMAN IDEAS

The Romans followed and improved upon many of the ideas put forward by Hippocrates. Galen (c. AD 130-200) was a Roman physician, who was born at Pergamum in Asia Minor. He learned that the muscles are controlled by the brain from his work as a doctor to the gladiators' school in Pergamum. Galen later became personal doctor to five of the Roman emperors.

Galen wrote medical works which covered 500 years of study by doctors of Greece and Rome as well as his own findings. He made many mistakes in his own theories because he did not base his arguments on observation of human

ACUPUNCTURE

The Chinese believe that the body contains twelve channels through which the life force 'chi' flows. Each channel is associated with a particular organ of the body. One way to stimulate the flow of chi (shown in red) along the channels is by acupuncture. This involves inserting special needles at certain points along the channels. Acupuncturists use a map of the body with the acupuncture points marked on it (see right). Each point is related to a particular part of the body or to a certain disorder. Acupuncture has been shown to work well for certain ailments and this method of treatment has become popular in the West.

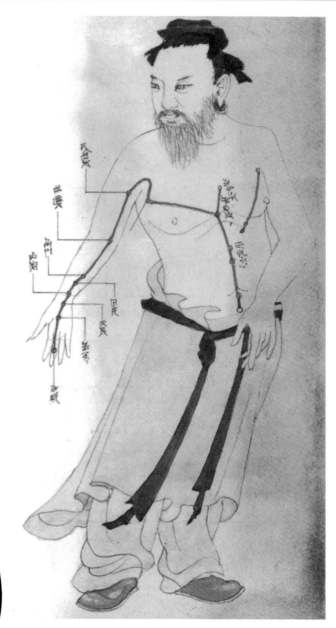

▽ *The Chinese symbol of yin and yang.*

patients. For example, he thought that the blood passed from one side of the heart to the other but did not realize that it circulated around the body. However, his skill in putting forward his arguments meant that his theories were not challenged for hundreds of years and remained the basis of medical thought for 1,500 years after his death.

IDEAS FROM THE EAST

As with all other aspects of their early civilization, the Chinese developed their medical ideas independently of anyone else. By the sixth century AD, the Chinese had a system of medicine which is still used today. This was the theory of 'yin and yang'. The Chinese believe that the two opposite forces of yin and yang dominate the world. These forces have to

△ *Medieval hospitals were run by nuns and monks. Generally, they were considered places to die, as anyone ill enough to go to hospital was unlikely to live.*

be balanced for good health. Each organ of the body is either yin or yang, and different circumstances and forces can influence the balance of yin and yang in the body. An imbalance leads to illness.

The Chinese also believe that a life force, known as 'chi', flows through the body and that this flow must be steady. Many types of Chinese medicine, including acupuncture, are concerned with balancing yin and yang and maintaining a steady flow of chi. Herbs, massage and other forms of natural treatment are used instead of drugs. These forms of medicine are 'holistic', that is they aim to treat the whole body rather than just the affected part.

MEDIEVAL MEDICINE

Doctors in the west continued to influence each other but knew nothing of the Chinese approach. After the fall of Rome in the fifth century AD, there was

no medical training in Europe, but the Arabs studied and translated many Greek manuscripts, making useful additions of their own. Ar-Razi (AD 865–925), chief physician at the hospital in Baghdad, was the first to distinguish between smallpox and measles. The medical works of the Persian writer Ibn Sina (AD 980–1037) were compulsory reading for European medical students until about 1650.

Medical teaching in Europe was revived in the tenth century, and Latin translations of the medical classics were made from the Arab works. Doctors still followed the teachings of Galen and Ibn Sina until the sixteenth century when there was a demand for them to start looking for themselves instead of

EARLY OPERATIONS

In the sixteenth century, doctors knew so little about the workings of the human body that internal operations were hardly ever attempted. Amputating or cutting off an infected limb was the most common operation. There were no anaesthetics in those days and the patient had to be held down while the limb was sawn off. Many patients either died from the shock of the operation or from infections caused by unhygenic conditions. The stump of the amputated limb was sealed with red-hot iron or boiling pitch to stop the bleeding.

The best surgeon of the time was Ambroise Paré (1517–90), a Frenchman who was surgeon-general to the armies of three French kings. Paré learned from the wounded soldiers he had to treat and operate on. He introduced new and more effective surgical instruments and a new way of stopping bleeding by tying up the arteries on the stump of an amputated limb. Paré also designed an artificial hand with fingers that moved by springs and small wheels. It was so effective that a soldier could grasp the reins of his horse with the fingers.

slavishly following the words of the ancients. This meant dissecting bodies to find out how they worked.

In 1543, a young Belgian named Andreas Vesalius (1514–64) published the first work on human anatomy based on careful observation of the dissected human body. The work of Vesalius was not really appreciated during his lifetime. People still continued to cling to the theories of Galen. After trying unsuccessfully to promote his teachings, Vesalius gave up and burned all his unpublished manuscripts. But his work was an important step forward. The medical world was ready to move on to finding out for itself, a process that has been continued ever since.

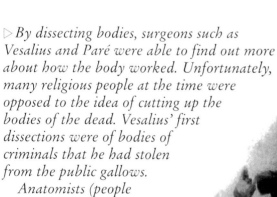

▷ *By dissecting bodies, surgeons such as Vesalius and Paré were able to find out more about how the body worked. Unfortunately, many religious people at the time were opposed to the idea of cutting up the bodies of the dead. Vesalius' first dissections were of bodies of criminals that he had stolen from the public gallows.*

Anatomists (people who study the inside of human bodies) were regarded with deep suspicion by most people until well into the nineteenth century.

MODERN MEDICINE

Today, doctors can prevent or cure diseases which were once major killers. Every day, surgeons carry out operations that only a few years ago would have seemed like miracles.

n 1980, an amazing news story was broadcast all around the world. Smallpox had been conquered! There had been no new cases anywhere in the world for three years. For centuries, smallpox was a major killer disease. It spread rapidly and uncontrollably. Doctors knew of no medicine that would cure it. Not everyone who caught smallpox died, though millions did. Victims who survived were left with the scars of the smallpox sores all over their bodies,

reminding them of their suffering for the rest of their lives.

The story of how smallpox was conquered is just one example of how medical and scientific research has improved the lives of everyone living today. The good news of 1980 began about 200 years earlier in the little town of Berkeley in England. The town's doctor, Edward Jenner (1749–1823), had

△ *In the late nineteenth century, people who worked with cows often fell victim to cowpox, a disease which seemed to stop them from getting smallpox.*

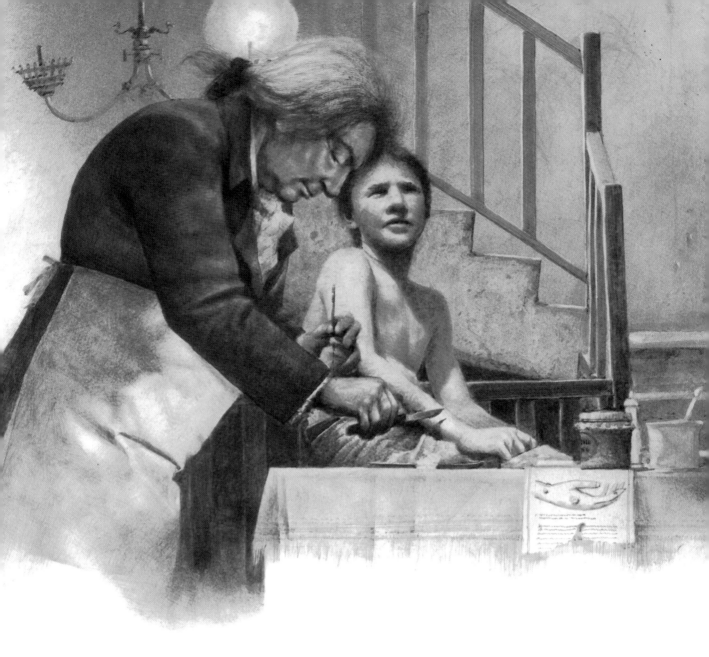

heard local people say that people who had suffered from cowpox, a mild disease which was caught from cattle, seemed afterwards to be protected from catching the much more serious smallpox. It was already known that people who survived smallpox, although they had to live with its scars, could not catch it again.

JENNER TAKES A CHANCE

Edward Jenner's idea was that if people could be deliberately infected with cowpox, this might protect them from smallpox in the future. In May 1796, he had the chance to try his idea out.

△ *Jenner's experiment with young James Phipps was a tremendous risk, but it paid off, saving the lives of millions of people.*

Sarah Nelmes, a local dairymaid, came to him with cowpox. He took scrapings from Sarah's cowpox sores, and used them to inoculate eight-year-old James Phipps. Now Jenner had to discover whether James would catch smallpox. In July 1797, the doctor inoculated him with smallpox.

It must have been an anxious wait to see if James developed smallpox, but Jenner's idea was proved correct. The

earlier cowpox inoculation prevented smallpox from taking hold.

Jenner's work had impressed the British royal family, and they supported him in setting up a programme of smallpox vaccination in London. In the first 18 months, from 1803 to 1804, vaccinations were given to about 12,000 people and the number of deaths from smallpox fell from over 2,000 to about 600. Soon afterwards, European countries began to make vaccination compulsory, and as medical services spread throughout the world, so too did the news about vaccination. The United Nations funded the last great programme of vaccination in Africa that resulted in the final conquest of the disease in 1980.

HOW THE BODY WORKS

Edward Jenner's work on smallpox was part of a more scientific approach to health problems which was taking over from the superstition and ignorance of the past. Little was known about how the body works or how disease spreads. Vesalius had been one of the first scientists to study the human body in the sixteenth century. When he became a professor at Padua University in Italy, he began a study of the body by dissecting the corpses of executed prisoners.

His drawings and charts identifying the functions of bones, muscles, the nervous system and other organs were published, but he met great opposition from the Roman Catholic Church and was forced out of his job. His books remained, and became textbooks for later generations of scientists, doctors and surgeons.

▷ *It was not until the sixteenth and seventeenth centuries, when doctors began to dissect and study corpses, that they really began to understand how the human body works.*

One of these was an Englishman, William Harvey (1578–1657), who studied at Padua where Vesalius had taught. Harvey returned to England to practise as a doctor in London, and it was there that he began to study the circulation of the blood. Before Harvey's time, no one really understood how the heart pumps blood round the body. His discoveries, published in 1628, led doctors to a completely new understanding of the body and of how diseases spread in it.

William Harvey's work was based on patient observation and experiment, and other doctors adopted his scientific methods. Harvey's message was that study led to understanding, and in the eighteenth century there was a growth in the number of medical schools in centres such as Edinburgh. Edward Jenner attended one of these, at St George's Hospital in London, from 1770 to 1773.

DETECTIVE WORK

Sometimes, advances resulted from investigations which were more like detective work than medicine. One of the greatest scourges of the nineteenth century was cholera, a disease that was almost always fatal within a few days. An epidemic of cholera spread across the world, starting in China in 1826. By 1830, it had reached Russia and then spread westwards through Europe, killing millions. There were outbreaks in Britain in 1832, 1848 and 1854.

No one knew what caused cholera or how it spread. One theory was that it was carried on the wind and was therefore unavoidable. However, some doctors noticed that it was most common among poor people, living in overcrowded homes with poor sanitation and communal water supplies.

▽ *Modern medicine, with its scientific basis seems a long way from traditional remedies, but today both forms of treatment are often used side by side.*

▽ *In the nineteenth century, people began to realize that the poor housing and sanitation in overcrowded cities was a major cause of disease.*

The truth was proved once and for all in 1854 when an English doctor, John Snow (1813–58), painstakingly traced the source of a cholera outbreak in central London. He found that almost all the victims were members of families that took their water supply from a particular street pump. When the pump handle was removed, the outbreak began to fade.

It was found later that the water in the pump had been contaminated by cholera-infected sewage. This striking example showed how the way people lived led to poor health. It was the start of improvements in public health, including better housing, clean water supplies and the proper disposal of sewage. In many countries, these aims have not yet been achieved, and cholera is still a threat.

LOOKING AND LISTENING

Another development in the nineteenth century was the increased use of instruments to study disease and diagnose illness. The earliest of these was the microscope, invented in the Netherlands round about 1590. In the 1650s, Anton van Leeuwenhoek (1632–1723) began making microscopes which enabled him to study blood vessels, muscle fibres and the layers of the skin. He also discovered the existence of micro-organisms in human tissue. Few doctors recognized the significance of Leeuwenhoek's work at the time, but two centuries later it became the basis of a new wave of progress in medical technology.

The microscope was to prove invaluable in medical research, but there were also a number of new instruments to help the doctor's everyday work in the surgery. These helped to form a general view of the patient's health as well as to identify particular health problems.

A French doctor, René Laennec (1781–1826) was the inventor of the medical instrument we are all familiar with, the stethoscope. Laennec discovered that a rolled-up piece of paper helped him hear his patients' heartbeats more clearly, and he developed a wooden tube with a sound-collector at one end and an ear-piece at the other. This type of stethoscope became popular from the 1830s until it was followed twenty years later by the instrument used today, with a flexible tube and two ear-pieces.

TAKING THE TEMPERATURE

The thermometer was another instrument that came into use in the nineteenth century. It had been invented over 200 years earlier, but the thermometer used until 1867 was a clumsy instrument 30 centimetres long, which took 20 minutes to register a temperature. An English doctor, Thomas Allbutt (1836–1925), invented a shorter version which took only five minutes to register.

By the end of the nineteenth century, doctors had an instrument called a 'sphygmomanometer', for measuring blood pressure. A rubber cuff was fitted round the upper arm and inflated with a rubber bulb. The pressure of air needed to stop the circulation in the arm was measured by a tube of mercury.

Instruments were also developed in the nineteenth century to enable doctors to see inside the patient's body. The first was the 'ophthalmoscope', which gave a good view of the inner eye, invented by a German doctor, Hermann von Helmholtz (1821–94) in 1851. Effective instruments, called 'endoscopes', to examine internal organs had to await the invention of the electric light bulb in the 1880s. More recently, the techniques of endoscopy have been transformed again with the use of fibre optic tubes which transmit pictures to television screens from inside the body.

THE 'MAGICAL' X-RAY

Of all the pieces of diagnostic equipment adopted in modern medicine, one of the most important followed the discovery of X-rays by a German physicist, Wilhelm von Roentgen (1845–1923). He discovered in 1895 that X-rays could be used to take photographs of the inside of a patient's body. This discovery enabled doctors to study, for example, the condition of a patient's lungs or how a bone has been broken. X-ray machines were adopted with enthusiasm by doctors, and have since proved invaluable in diagnosing and

△ *Nineteenth-century stethoscopes.*

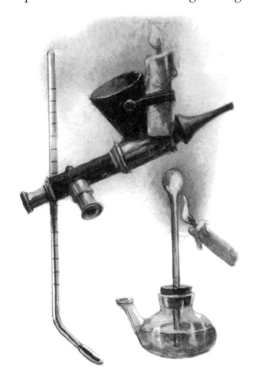

△ *Early thermometers and endoscopes.*

△ *Rapid surgery was important on the battlefields of the nineteenth century.*

treating diseases such as tuberculosis and cancer, as well as in general surgery.

ON THE OPERATING TABLE

Today, surgical operations are fairly straightforward, but it was a very different story 200 years ago. If you went to the dentist, he pulled out your infected teeth with pliers and you had to put up with the pain. More serious surgery was carried out only if there was no other way to save a patient's life. Even so, many patients died during the

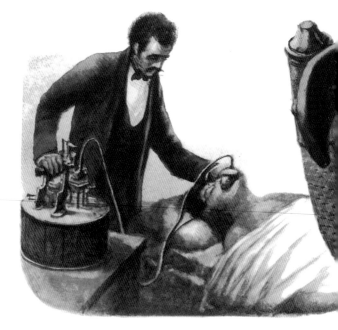

operation. There was no way of killing the pain of the operation. Patients were held down, screaming, while it was going on. All that surgeons could do to help was to try to get the job over as quickly as possible.

However, that was not the end. Often, the wounds from the operation became infected and the patient died of blood poisoning. The reason why infection spread in the body so easily after an operation was not properly understood.

The first improvement was the introduction of anaesthetics to make the patient unconscious while surgery was being carried out. This was not only a

question of making operations less painful. If the patient was unconscious, the surgeon could take more time and work more accurately. Problems such as the loss of blood during an operation could be overcome more easily. Longer operations could be carried out, and this increased the range of health problems that surgery could treat.

TREATING THE WOUNDED

Pressure to improve standards of surgery came in the nineteenth century from an unexpected source. It was a time of savage wars throughout Europe and of the American Civil War. New weapons

ANAESTHETICS

The first surgeon to use ether as an anaesthetic was a young doctor in Jefferson, Georgia, USA, in 1842. Crawford Long (1815–78) removed a tumour from the neck of a patient after making him unconscious. Two years later, a Vermont dentist, Horace Wells (1815–48) used nitrous oxide, or 'laughing-gas', to extract teeth painlessly.

James Simpson (1811–70) was a Scottish doctor who, in 1847, started using ether as an anaesthetic for mothers in childbirth. He was not satisfied, and began the search for something better. The answer he found was chloroform. Many people were opposed to the use of anaesthetics in childbirth. However, opposition faded after Queen Victoria (1819–1901) agreed to have chloroform during the birth of her eighth child in 1853.

△ *Nineteenth-century ether inhaler.*

LOUIS PASTEUR

Most nineteenth-century surgeons thought that their patients' deaths were caused by a mysterious poison in the air. Understanding of disease took a huge leap forward when Frenchman Louis Pasteur (1822–95) worked out his 'germ theory' showing that infections were caused by micro-organisms called bacteria.

Pasteur was trained as a chemist, and in 1854 he was appointed dean of the faculty of sciences at Lille University. He began to study micro-organisms as part of an investigation into why wine went sour and food went bad. He discovered that bacteria which cause decay in food can be killed by heating it. This process, still used to stop milk going sour, is called 'pasteurization' after its inventor. It was only afterwards that he went on to apply his findings to human medicine.

Later, Pasteur developed a vaccine against anthrax, a deadly disease passed from cattle to humans, and, perhaps most spectacularly, a vaccine for rabies, which is passed on if someone is bitten by an infected animal, such as a dog or fox.

meant that more soldiers were wounded on the battlefield. Many soldiers were left to die, and even those whowere given medical help did not survive long. It was this situation that led to the foundation of the Red Cross movement after a particularly cruel battle between French and Austrian troops at Solferino in northern Italy in 1859.

It led also to the realization that many of the lives of the wounded could be saved if their injuries were treated immediately, before fatal infection set in. But how could infection be stopped?

KEEPING CLEAN

The pioneer work of the French chemist Louis Pasteur on his 'germ theory' showed that infection was caused by bacteria, which were micro-organisms similar to those observed by van Leeuwenhoek many years before. A British surgeon, Joseph Lister (1827–1912), began to apply Pasteur's theory to the operating theatre at Edinburgh Medical School, where he was a professor of surgery.

Lister insisted that the operating theatre and its equipment must be scrupulously clean. He also made use of the discovery by another professor, F. Grace Calvert (1819–73), that phenol, or carbolic acid, was effective in slowing the process of decay. Lister used a spray to create a mist of carbolic acid around patients' wounds during operations, and also used carbolic acid to clean and dress the wounds.

The result was a dramatic cut in the number of patients who suffered from infection after operations. This also meant that many limbs which would previously have had to be amputated could be saved.

PREVENTING INFECTION

The lasting importance of Lister's methods lay in his insistence on germ-free conditions in the operating theatre. The use of carbolic acid was soon abandoned because it was found to irritate patients' wounds.

Alternative ways were found of preventing wounds from becoming infected. Surgeons, who had previously worn ordinary clothes to carry out operations, began to wear gowns, masks and caps. These could be sterilized after use under steam pressure in an 'autoclave', which first came into use in hospitals in 1886. It was similar to a pressure cooker and based on a much earlier invention by a French scientist, Denis Papin (1647–1712). The autoclave was also used to sterilize dressings and the surgeon's instruments.

△ *Reformer Florence Nightingale (1820–1910) helped to improve the appalling conditions in nineteenth-century hospitals and founded the modern nursing profession. Her patients gave her the nickname 'the Lady with the Lamp' because she would wander the wards at night with her lamp, checking to see that all the patients were comfortable and had everything they needed.*

Another improvement in operating techniques came in 1890, when an American surgeon began to use thin rubber gloves which could be thrown away after the operation.

◁ *Joseph Lister and his carbolic acid spray.*

SPARE PARTS

There were improvements during the nineteenth century even for those patients who had to have limbs amputated. 'Wooden legs' had been used for centuries, since at least 5000 BC, but until the nineteenth century they were crude, unsightly, and had no joints. There was an important change in 1815 when an artificial leg jointed at the knee and ankle, was produced for the Marquis of Anglesey (1768–1854), who had lost a leg at the battle of Waterloo.

By the end of the century the improved limb was available to all, not just to the rich. There was a similar improvement in artificial arms, harnessed to the body and jointed at the elbow.

FALSE TEETH

Alongside improvements in medical care for the seriously ill, the nineteenth century also saw more attention for more minor health problems such as teeth and eye disorders. The invention of anaesthetics made a visit to the dentist a far less painful experience, and new technology brought benefits to people who had to wear false teeth.

False teeth, made of ivory and held together with gold wires and plates, had been available for centuries for those who could afford them. They were fitted by taking measurements inside the mouth, which was difficult to do at all

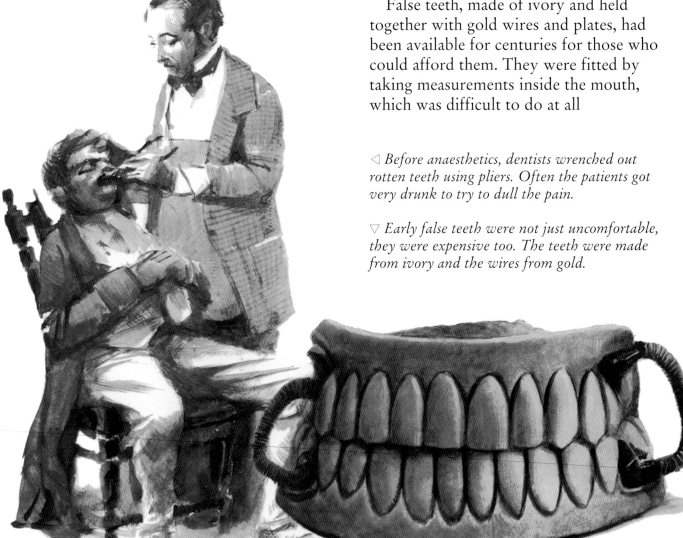

◁ Before anaesthetics, dentists wrenched out rotten teeth using pliers. Often the patients got very drunk to try to dull the pain.

▽ Early false teeth were not just uncomfortable, they were expensive too. The teeth were made from ivory and the wires from gold.

accurately. In the eighteenth century, dentists began to take wax casts of the teeth. Plaster moulds were then made from the casts and used as a pattern, and this improved the fitting.

However, the real breakthrough, which made false teeth a possibility for poorer people, came in 1844 with the invention by Charles Goodyear (1800–60) of vulcanite, a kind of hard rubber. This proved to be a cheap and comfortable material for the dental plate, to which porcelain teeth were attached.

TOOTH-BRUSHING

The causes of tooth decay were not properly understood until late in the nineteenth century. People expected to lose their teeth quite early in life, often in their thirties, and it was normal for them to have complete sets of false teeth, top and bottom. Many regarded their natural teeth as a nuisance and a source of pain which was best avoided by replacing them with false ones. In 1884, research in Berlin, Germany, showed that tooth decay is caused by bacteria feeding on acids in the mouth. This discovery led dentists to emphasize the importance of regular brushing after meals, especially for children whose teeth are still developing. Although it has taken a century to achieve, the teeth of people in the Western world are more healthy and less prone to decay than they have ever been.

TREATING POOR EYESIGHT

Poor sight was another health problem that most people believed just had to be accepted. Spectacles had been used for centuries, but they were expensive and were little more than magnifying lenses mounted in frames. In the nineteenth century, opticians began to test the sight of each eye with frames containing trial

△ *Spectacles were usually just magnifying glasses of different strengths, not made accurately for each particular patient's vision, as they are today.*

lenses. In this way, pairs of spectacles could be prescribed in which the particular sight problem of each eye was corrected. The invention of the ophthalmoscope also enabled the interior of the eyes to be examined for more serious defects.

ACHIEVEMENT

By the end of the nineteenth century, doctors had a far better idea of what causes disease, and how it can be prevented or cured, than they had had a hundred years earlier. Fewer diseases were fatal, surgery was no longer so risky and patients suffered less pain. The stage was set for even more hopeful developments in the twentieth century, but we have all benefited from the work of the scientists, researchers and doctors of the nineteenth century.

FIND OUT SOME MORE

After you have read about the ideas and inventions in this book, you may want to find out some more information about them. There are lots of books devoted to specific topics, such as religion or medicine, so that you can discover more facts. All over Britain and Ireland, you can see historical sites and visit museums that contain historical artefacts that will tell you more about the subjects that interest you. The books, sites and museums listed below cover some of the most important topics in this book. They are just a start!

GENERAL INFORMATION

BOOKS

These books all present a large number of inventions of all different kinds:

Oxford Illustrated Encyclopedia of Invention and Technology edited by Sir Monty Finniston (Oxford University Press, 1992)

Usborne Illustrated Handbook of Invention and Discovery by Struan Reid (Usborne, 1986)

Invention by Lionel Bender (Dorling Kindersley, 1986)

The Way Things Work by David Macaulay (Dorling Kindersley, 1988)

Key Moments in Science and Technology by Keith Wicks (Hamlyn, 1999)

A History of Invention by Trevor I. Williams (Little Brown, 1999)

WEBSITE

For information on many different inventions, visit: http://inventors.about.com

MUSEUMS

Many large museums contain interesting artefacts related to people of the past, and some have collections that may be more specifically about some of the themes covered in this book.

To find out more about the museums in your area, ask in your local library or tourist information office, or look in the telephone directory.

A useful guide is *Museums & Galleries in Great Britain & Ireland* (British Leisure Publications, East Grinstead) which tells you about over 1,300 places to visit. For a good introduction to the subjects covered in this book, visit:

Science Museum, Exhibition Road, London SW7 www.sciencemuseum.org.uk

For displays and information about many of the earliest ideas and inventions, go to:

British Museum, Great Russell Street, London WC1 www.britishmuseum.co.uk

These books include background information on early human development:

The Dawn of Man by Steve Parker (Eagle Editions, 1998)

Man's Place in Evolution (Natural History Museum, 1980)

The Earliest Civilizations by Margaret Oliphant (Simon & Schuster, 1991)

EARLY RELIGIONS

There are many standing stones and barrows (prehistoric burial mounds) all over the country. You can find out about them in your local library or tourist information centre.

SITES

Stonehenge, near Amesbury, Wiltshire
   A world-famous prehistoric monument.
   www.english-heritage.org.uk/stonehenge

Avebury Stone Circle, Avebury, Wiltshire
   A huge, impressive stone circle surrounds the village, with an interesting museum.
   www.nationaltrust.org.uk

Beaghmore Stone Circles,
   Beaghmore, Co. Tyrone, Ireland

Stenness Standing Stones,
   Finstown, Orkney

CAVE PAINTINGS

BOOKS

Prehistoric People by Tim Wood (Franklin Watts, 1980)

SITES

To see the best cave paintings, you will have to visit caves in France and Spain. Some of the finest are at **Lascaux** in the Dordogne, and **Altamira** in Spain. For lots of information about Lascaux, visit: www.culture.fr/culture/arcnat/lascaux/en

MEDICINE

BOOKS

Surgery by Tony Hooper (Simon & Schuster, 1992)

MUSEUMS

For a fascinating journey through the history of medicine, visit:

Science Museum, London (address above)

Old Operating Theatre, Museum & Herb Garret,
   9a, Thomas Street, London SE1
   www.thegarret.org.uk

The Jenner Museum, Church Lane, High Street, Berkeley, Gloucestershire
   www.jennermuseum.com

The Royal Museum of Scotland, Chambers Street, Edinburgh

INDEX

INDEX